完全さ

# Perfection

*First Edition*

# 10 Secrets to Successful Lean Manufacturing Implementation

PIETRO SAVO

Pietro Savo **Tradition Book**

© Pietro Savo **Tradition Book**

First Edition

Copyright Year: ©2006

Edited by P.B. Gorman
Cover Design and Interior Design by Rhiannon Dziemien

Copyright Notice by Pietro Savo.
All rights reserved. No part of this book may be reproduced, distributed, or transmitted in any form or by any means, including photocopying, recording, or other electronic or mechanical methods, without the prior written permission of publisher, except in the case of brief quotations embodied in critical reviews and certain other noncommercial uses permitted by copyright law.

For permission request, e-mail to publisher, PietroSavoUSA@aol.com, "Attention: Permissions coordinator."

Published By Pietro Savo **Tradition Book**
ISBN: 978-0-6151-6364-2

*To my children, **Bridget, Caitlin, Alicia, Daniel, Tiana,** and **Dante.***

*What I have learned from them is to ask questions like a child.*

**Pietro Savo** has a Masters of Aeronautical Science in Human Factors from Embry Riddle Aeronautical University and a Bachelor of Science in Business Administration from Sacred Heart University. Pietro holds a certificate from Tuck School of Business at Dartmouth College (Minority Business Executive Program) and from the Supplier Excellence Alliance (Operational Excellence Lean Manufacturing Consultant). Pietro is the author of "Root Cause Analysis System for Problem Solving and Problem Avoidance." He is also a licensed pilot. Pietro and his wife Pat live in New Hampshire with their six children. He is currently restoring a two hundred thirty-seven year old antique home in his spare time.

**Perfection** begins with the simple belief that perfection is achievable and well within our reach. Creating a destiny that values the creation of perfection begins during our first heart beat. We soon breathe on our own and the journey to perfection becomes a race. A race that builds momentum until our journey finds us entering eternal life. Perfection begins with our spirit being renewed back into the image of God. Soon the perfection of our work becomes the most sought after value that we desire in our work place.

Achieving perfection in our work life has many common sense Lean Thinking tools available to ensure success. To guide our work lives to perfection, I developed the "10 Secrets to Successful Lean Manufacturing Implementation."

# 10 Secrets to Successful Lean Manufacturing Implementation

1 *Crazy About Kaizen!*

2 *Invest in the People*

3 *Certify your Suppliers*

4 *Live and Breathe the Customer's Desires*

5 *Value Stream Mapping (VSM)*

6 *Think Single Piece Flow*

7 *Perfection Comes From the Lessons Learned While Removing Imperfection*

8 *Communicate*

9 *Innovation with Common Sense*

10 *Kanban Like a Religion*

*Crazy About Kaizen!*

The meaning of Kaizen is slow but continuous improvement, doing "little things" better, setting and achieving ever-higher standards. Kaizen is an important part of the examination process for waste reduction. The 80/20 rule, eighty percent of waste is designed into the product and services. Conducting Kaizen during product and service development results in a "built in" efficient flow. Performing Kaizen during all the product's life inspires efficiency in legacy products and services. It is always productive to engage in Kaizen. Productive people are in motion; Kaizen fuels the motion one event at a time, creating the "go-and-do-it" attitude. Kaizen can inspire; however, true lean transformation does not happen in a day. It takes consistent and persistent willingness to change and improve. Too often, we lose sight of the fact that suitable change is considered work. Some say it is associated with the same level of effort that brought us to the current level of inefficiency in the first place. Kaizen fuels the "go-and-do-it" attitude because it transforms a culture that realizes "doing it" was better than simply talking about it.

Kaizen is Japanese for "change for the better" or "improvement," the English translation is "continuous improvement," or "continual improvement." When we focus on perfection the definition of Kaizen evolves and becomes "improvement in motion."

改善

# 2

*Invest in the People*

Invest in the culture changes around the people and the by-product becomes the "go-and-do-it" team!

Teach the value stream at all levels of an organization. People can be much like a radical undeveloped river flow after a sudden downburst of rain. When you plan for the downburst, what you get in return is a developed flow that is controlled and organized. A developed flow is less disruptive and has a greater efficiency that can be visually pleasing.

Investing in people is the greatest developed flow. People become part of the great successes when instilling the values and culture of continuous improvement are focused on developing talent and leadership, innovatively redeploying, and cross training. Incorporating value-added services, standardizing, and production methods creates a robust people infrastructure that is efficient, profitable, filled with quality, and is delivery driven.

# 3

*Certify your Suppliers*

Certify your supplier for purchased parts and materials and have them shipped directly to the point of use. Create a partnership of accountability at the supplier base. The question you should ask yourself is, "are my suppliers the best?" When they are certified to your high standards the answer is yes; this is important because these suppliers become an extension of your company.

Lean companies have cross-functional teams to certify suppliers. Lean companies create and use a certification process that challenges suppliers and makes them proud to be certified. Lean companies recognize certified suppliers publicly and award them plaques that can be proudly displayed.

The benefits are endless when the supplier is your partner. Your standards are shared across the supplier base. Everyone produces better products and services while cutting mistakes and alleviating confusion, which results in the creation of leaner operations.

*Live and Breathe the Customer's Desires*

Rule number one: the customer is king; without customers the other nine secrets to successful lean manufacturing implementation do not matter; any questions? The customer is always right; right or wrong is not a question. Keeping the customer satisfied and happy is your ultimate goal.

Customer alert people are…people who are dedicated to becoming World Class…in order to better serve their internal and external customers. A satisfied customer will keep coming back. It is easier to keep a customer than to have to find a new customer; any questions?

*Value
Stream
Mapping
(VSM)*

Value Stream Mapping is the most important tool that visually points to a business' critical areas in which we need to focus improvement solutions. This map helps you visualize flow. It cuts across all functions, departments, processes, etc. It shows issues in flow and excessive inventory and work in progress (WIP). It allows you to see waste and more. It also allows you to see the sources of waste.

Understanding the value stream contributes to waste reduction and efficiency improvement. Using Value Stream Mapping (VSM) you can picture the organizational layout. The layout must support the flow of work needed to support a truly Lean plan. Therefore, organizational imperfection becomes a visual reality that can be attacked using proven Lean methodology. Non-value added steps and non-value added portions of a business can now be visualized and non-value or waste can be removed.

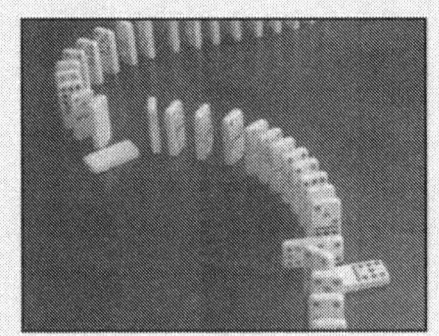

# 6

*Think Single Piece Flow*

Batches are a disease; vaccinate everyone against batches when possible. The transition from batch and queue to lean manufacturing involves converting to single piece flow. Going lean is all about cultural transformation. Everyone in the organization must change the way they have been doing things and embrace new process changes. Single Piece Flow (SPF) supports Just-in-Time, Toyota Production Systems, Lean Manufacturing, Theory of Constraints, and similar types of philosophies.

Symptoms suggesting that Single Piece Flow is needed include long delivery lead times, obsolete inventories, visible piles of large batches all with similar defects, low inventory turns, slow changeovers, and left-overs at the beginning and end of production runs.

# 動きの改善

*Perfection Comes From the Lessons Learned
While Removing Imperfection*

Face imperfection with open eyes and mind. An open mind understands that the best practices of lean thinking have not all been invented yet. Open eyes look for and recognize the variation that leads to imperfection. Perfection in lean production means there are endless opportunities for improving.

Lean thinking is a never-ending search for perfection. While perfection may never be fully achieved, its pursuit is a goal worth striving for because it energizes the constant vigilance against wasteful practices.

Communicate

Communicate, to share, and build an environment that fuels open discussions and trust in all direction. Both the single biggest hurdle and key reason for successful implementation of organizational change is communication.

Lean successes are credited to teams that promote communication and engagement at all levels. These teams contain energetic individuals with clear goals to build teams of people who inspire and energize associates at all levels. These values create diversity and encourage those who are smart, multidimensional global thinkers. Team diversity in communication is evident for lean successes when gaining multiple viewpoints and new ideas. As a whole, focus on doing everything simpler, better, and faster to fuel the advantages derived from excellent communication skills. You cannot communicate too much!

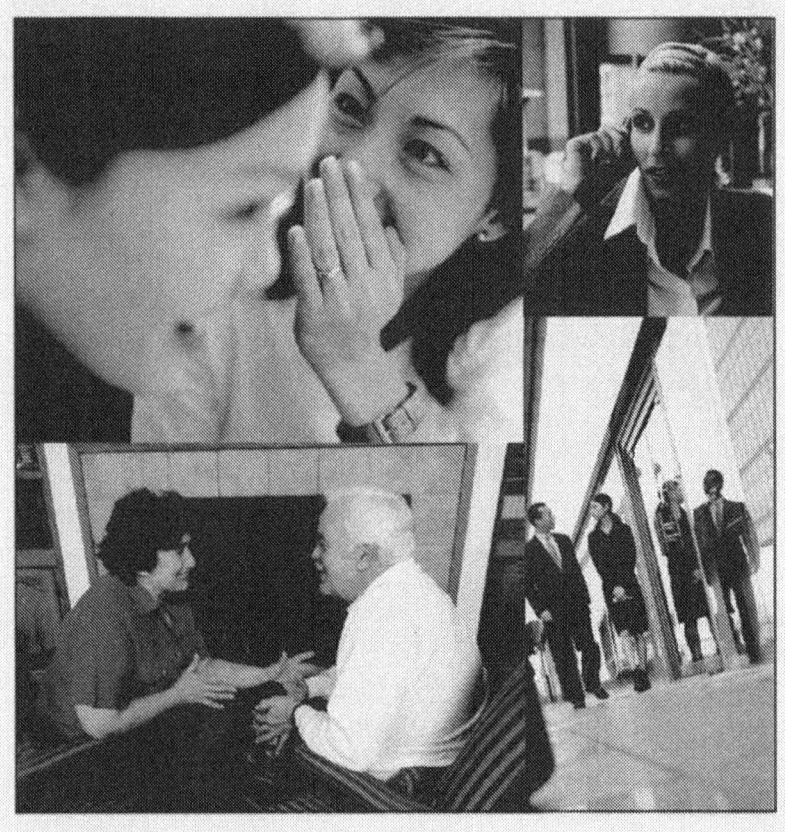

"We spent so much time perfecting the communications, we forgot the message."

*Innovation with Common Sense*

Innovation with common sense, keep it simple, complicated solutions need a translator. There is no shortage of books written about lean manufacturing and the value it can create by eliminating non-value processes. What some may call innovation, the lean world calls common sense.

Just imagine the improvements we could make if everything were made so simple everyone could understand it. Lean brings simplicity and common sense; it is an approach everyone can relate to that is both honest and simple!

*Kanban
Like a
Religion*

Kanban like a religion, make it second nature. Kan means "card" in Japanese, and the word "ban" means "signal." Kanban controls the work in process (WIP) between workstations using visual signals. Visual signals can take the form of color-coded cards, empty containers, empty floor spaces, and electronic signals.

There are three main types of kanbans. The production kanban is a communication to the supplier to produce parts. The withdrawal kanban is a communication to request a withdrawal of parts. A material kanban is a communication to trigger purchases. Therefore, nothing is made unless the downstream asks for it.

# カード信号

The
**"Go and Do It"**
attitude...

...the start of
perfection!

ISBN 978-0-6151-6364-2

www.ingramcontent.com/pod-product-compliance
Lightning Source LLC
Chambersburg PA
CBHW051718040426
42446CB00008B/955